Make School Meaningful— And Fun!

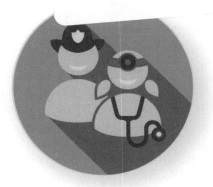

Roger C. Schank

Solution Tree | Press
a division of
Solution Tree

Copyright © 2016 by Solution Tree Press

All rights reserved, including the right of reproduction of this book in whole or in part in any form.

555 North Morton Street
Bloomington, IN 47404
800.733.6786 (toll free) / 812.336.7700
FAX: 812.336.7790
email: info@solution-tree.com
solution-tree.com

Printed in the United States of America

19 18 17 16 15   1 2 3 4 5

Library of Congress Control Number: 2015943625

ISBN: 978-1-942496-21-2 (perfect bound)

Solution Tree
Jeffrey C. Jones, CEO
Edmund M. Ackerman, President

Solution Tree Press
President: Douglas M. Rife
Senior Acquisitions Editor: Amy Rubenstein
Editorial Director: Lesley Bolton
Managing Production Editor: Caroline Weiss
Senior Production Editor: Christine Hood
Proofreader: Elisabeth Abrams
Text and Cover Designer: Rian Anderson
Compositors: Rachel Smith and Abigail Bowen

educa

WISSER MEMORIAL LIBRARY

LB 1628

.S33

2016

c. 1

Table of Contents

About the Author

 **Roger C. Schank** is one of the world's leading visionaries in artificial intelligence, learning theory, cognitive science, and the building of virtual learning environments. Early in his career, Schank was a professor at Stanford University and Yale University. Later, he held a chaired professorship at Northwestern University, where he established the Institute for the Learning Sciences. He is currently CEO and founder of Socratic Arts, a company whose goal is to design and implement learning-by-doing, story-centered curricula in schools, universities, and corporations.

To book Roger C. Schank for professional development, contact pd@solution-tree.com.

Preface

By Will Richardson

In the 1960s and 1970s, Penguin published a series of what it called *education specials*, short books from a variety of authors such as Neil Postman, Ivan Illich, Herb Kohl, Paulo Freire, Jonathan Kozol, and others. All told, there were more than a dozen works, and they were primarily edgy, provocative essays meant to articulate an acute dissatisfaction with the function of schools at the time. The titles reflected that and included books such as *The Underachieving School*, *Compulsory Mis-Education and the Community of Scholars*, *Teaching as a Subversive Activity*, *Deschooling Society*, and *School Is Dead*, to name a few. Obviously, the messages of these books were not subtle.

Progressive by nature, the authors generally saw their schools as unequal, undemocratic, and controlling places of conformity and indoctrination. They argued, mostly to nonlistening ears, that traditional school narratives were leaving their learners disengaged and lacking in creativity and curiosity, and the systems and structures of schools were deepening instead of ameliorating the inequities in society. A number of the authors argued that universal schooling was a pipe dream from both economic and political perspectives, and schools, if they were to remain, needed to be rethought from the ground up.

Reading many of these works now, it's hard not to be struck by how precisely they describe many of the realities of today's world. It's inarguable that an education in the United States (and elsewhere) remains vastly unequal among socioeconomic groups and various races and ethnicities. The systems that drove schools years ago prevail and, in many cases, are less and less economically viable by the day. By and large, education is something still organized, controlled, and delivered by the institution; very little agency or autonomy is afforded to the learner over his or her own learning. Decades of reform efforts guided principally by politicians and businesspeople have failed to enact the types of widespread changes that those Penguin authors and many others felt were needed for schools to serve every learner equally and adequately in preparing him or her for the world that lies ahead.

It's the "world that lies ahead" that is the focus of this book, part of the *Solutions for Modern Learning* series. Let us say up front that we in no way assume that these books will match the intellectual heft of those writers in the Penguin series (though we hope to come close). However, we aspire to reignite or perhaps even start some important conversations about change in schools, given the continuing longstanding challenges from decades past as well as the modern contexts of a highly networked, technology-packed, fast-changing world whose future looks less predictable by the minute.

Changes in technology since the early 1990s, and specifically, the Internet, have had an enormous impact on how we communicate, create, and most importantly, learn. Nowhere have those effects been felt more acutely than with our learners, most of whom have never known a world without the Internet. In almost all areas of life, in almost every institution and society, the effects of ubiquitously connected technologies we now carry with us in our backpacks and back pockets have been profound, creating amazing opportunities and complex challenges, both of which have been hard to foresee. In no uncertain terms, the world has changed and continues to change quickly and drastically.

Yet, education has remained fairly steadfast, pushing potentially transformative learning devices and programs to the edges, never allowing them to penetrate to the core of learning in schools. Learning in schools looks, sounds, and feels pretty much like it did in the 1970s, if not in the early 1900s.

Here's the problem: increasingly, for those who have the benefit of technology devices and access to the Internet, learning outside of school is more profound, relevant, and long lasting than learning inside the classroom. Connected learners of all ages have agency and autonomy that are stripped from them as they enter school. In a learning context, this is no longer the world that schools were built for, and in that light, it's a pretty good bet that a fundamental redefinition of school is imminent.

While some would like to see schools done away with completely, we believe schools can play a crucially important role in the lives of our youth, the fabric of our communities, and the functioning of our nations. But moving forward, we believe schools can only play these roles if we fully understand and embrace the new contexts that the modern world offers for learning and education. This is not just about equal access to technology and the Internet, although that's a good start. This is about seeing our purpose and our practice through a different lens that understands the new literacies, skills, and dispositions that students need to flourish in a networked world. Our hope is that the books in the *Solutions for Modern Learning* series make that lens clearer and more widespread.

Chapter 1
Thinking About Student Goals

*Give the pupils something to do, not something to learn;
and the doing is of such a nature as to demand thinking;
learning naturally results.*

—John Dewey

In 1910, John Dewey tried to convince Americans that school needed to be more than the filling of an empty vessel. Many philosophers before him—Plato, Locke, Hume, Kant, and others—pushed hard for the idea that people learn by doing, not by listening. But unfortunately, at more or less the same time that Dewey was promoting his ideas about progressive education, far more powerful forces were at work.

In 1892, the president of Harvard University, Charles Eliot, and his friends decided to create a high school curriculum for the entire United States to follow. Dewey's ideas were ignored. The 1892 curriculum has now been around for so long that it seems there is no changing it. This is in part because many vested interests in education want the curriculum to stay exactly the same, except with more testing (Dexter, 1906; Hertzberg, 1988; National Education Association of the United States, 1894).

In today's schools, students do not learn by doing, and they learn exactly what Eliot decided that they should learn. Learning by doing requires something you are trying to accomplish (like riding a bike) and gradually getting better at it. Instead, as Eliot suggested, school is about academic subjects. Success means memorizing facts. There is no doing.

In *Experience and Education*, Dewey (1938) writes about the high school curriculum, which is dominated by facts and truths that all students must learn.

> There is no such thing as educational value in the abstract. The notion that some subjects and methods and that acquaintance with certain facts and truths possess educational value in and of themselves is the reason why traditional education reduced the material of education so largely to a diet of predigested materials. (p. 46)

The Common Core State Standards, the latest in reform/testing movements, is an attempt to ensure that the same 1892 curriculum is taught to every student, regardless of his or her interests, personal needs, or future aspirations. In the words of Bill Gates: "Common Core is 'a technocratic issue,' akin to making sure all states use the same type of electrical outlet" (as cited in Simon, 2014). Gates continues with this analogy:

> "Standardization is especially important to allow for innovation in the classroom," said Gates, who used an analogy of electrical outlets. "If you have fifty different plug types, appliances wouldn't be available and would be very expensive. . . . But once an electric outlet becomes standardized, many companies can design appliances and competition ensues, creating variety and better prices for consumers." (as cited in Layton, 2014)

In other words, Gates wants to plug every student into a place where he or she can work as an effective part of the machine. No differences will be tolerated. Curiously, this was exactly the plan in

1900 when United States schools were designed. The goal then was to create compliant factory workers.

In 1905, Ellwood Cubberley—the future dean of education at Stanford—wrote that schools should be factories in which raw products (children) are formed into finished products. Children should be manufactured like nails, and government and industry are the ones who provide specifications for manufacturing (Sears & Henderson, 1957).

Of course, Dewey was out of step with the forces of his time in education. This would be fine if we could say that was then, but education is different now. However, with the exception that we have no jobs for compliant factory workers, education doesn't look much different. Schools are still oppressive places, and the curriculum is exactly the same as it was.

What can we build to replace this ancient idea of education based on memorization, dull repetitive work, and testing? Why can't we build something new? Once again, Dewey (1916) sees the path: "Were all instructors to realize that the quality of mental process, not the production of correct answers, is the measure of educative growth something hardly less than a revolution in teaching would be worked" (p. 207).

There is no reason to make students memorize historical events or physics formulas. There is no reason to teach them to balance chemical equations. They needn't read Dickens, and they don't have to understand Shakespeare. They don't need to know the Pythagorean theorem, nor must we ram calculus down their throats.

I know these are strong statements, and many who read this will find them objectionable. Many readers are likely to have graduated college and will have spent time doing everything I just said wasn't necessary. Of course, students gain knowledge from studying what we teach in high school. But what do they lose?

For one thing, students lose interest. They may like some of the subjects they study, but they rarely like all of them. They lose the possibility of attaining practical skills because no one ever teaches them any. Adults have plenty of time to discover Dickens. And if they become curious about the social conditions in England in the 1800s, they can always find out on their own. In high school, I was assigned to read *A Tale of Two Cities*. I had no idea what it was about. Wasn't there anything else, anything more relevant, that I could study?

We can help and encourage students to learn what they want to learn. We can offer choices and make them as appealing as possible, so students will want to try new activities and experiences. This is what education should be about. Now is the time. The technology we need to accomplish that goal is here.

If we are going to design new curricula for K–12, it is reasonable to ask what should drive the selection of those curricula. In 1892, the driver was the desires of elite universities. Unfortunately, this is still true today.

What Harvard Wants

The following excerpt is taken directly from the Harvard University (n.d.) website. You may choose to take the term *recommend* here lightly; you might get into Harvard without having done all that's described, but it would be a very special case.

> We hope you will read our thoughts about choosing high school courses that will provide a strong base for a liberal arts education. But in summary, we recommend:
>
> - The study of English for four years: close and extensive reading of the classics of the world's literature
>
> - Four years of a single foreign language
>
> - The study of history for at least two, and preferably three years: American history,

European history, and one additional
advanced history course

- The study of mathematics for four years . . .
- The study of science for four years: physics,
  chemistry, and biology, and preferably one of
  these at an advanced level
- Frequent practice in the writing of expository
  prose

Children have goals of their own, of course. These goals don't necessarily include studying physics or learning European history. The goals children actually have develop over time in response to their reactions to the world around them. Very young children typically have the goal of taking shiny objects and putting them in their mouths, for example. They may learn over time that this is not a great idea, or they might continue to do this over their lifetime. But, one way or another, children observe the world and react to it. They develop new goals every day.

For example, a child typically only wants to play soccer if he or she sees someone (maybe an older sibling, a parent, or other children in the park) playing soccer or if someone encourages him or her to play soccer. These goals don't just spontaneously come to mind. The major determinants of a child's goals are his or her parents, who regularly try to set goals for their child partly based on their own basic desires and feelings.

This brings us to the great conundrum of curriculum design. Should curriculum designers be the ones to decide what students need to learn? As a society, this idea is never up for debate. *Adults know what children should learn, and children will be taught those subjects.* This simple sentence is what is wrong with today's schools. The idea is so taken for granted that you may never have heard anyone suggest that maybe the schools and the parents have no idea what they are doing.

What Parents Want

Most of children's lives, adults set goals for them. Parents want their children to join the team, get A's in school, and get along with their siblings. Teachers want children to behave in class and do well on the tests. The government tells children that its leaders are the smartest in the world, and the country in which they live is the best. This is how every child grows up, receiving core beliefs from the adults he or she spends time with and, because these are often presented without alternatives, simply believing them.

This isn't exactly bad. When your dad tells you the sun will rise tomorrow, he is right. When your mom tells you that if you are nice to your sister, then your sister will be nice to you, she is likely right as well. By and large, most of what parents teach their children is worth knowing and worth believing, but not all of it.

Parents might have mistaken beliefs. They might think something is true that isn't. Parents typically believe that the subjects they learned in school are just fine. This is a classic case of cognitive dissonance. They worked hard on boring stuff and so should their children. Typically included in parental beliefs, however, are goals that are worth striving for. The problem is that while parents may think their children believe in these goals, their children may not actually have those goals for themselves.

Parents often don't know their children very well. They might say to their child, "You should be an engineer," and the child may accept this without really knowing what an engineer does. That may be the wrong course of action for a particular child given who he or she actually is. Determining who you are and what goals really work for you is a big part of growing up. Everyone seems to know what you should do except *you*. Children need to find out for themselves. Do children decide to go to high school? What are their educational goals in high school? The fact that these seem like funny questions says a lot.

Similarly, when a student plans on going to college, how exactly does that happen? What is the advantage of going to college? What about the money involved? What are the alternatives? Who sets that goal? Typically, children do not suddenly come up with the idea of going to college. *It is expected of them. Everyone is going. They can't succeed without college.* Beliefs like this are simply inculcated into children from various sources, and they drive a child's decision making about everything. For every goal a child has, there may be a better alternative he or she never even considered because no one thought to mention it.

My son always knew his own goals. When he was ten years old, he was fascinated with subways. He checked out the subway system of every city he visited as a teenager. When he went to college, he asked me what I thought his major should be. I said, "Subways." (He already had chosen to go to college in New York City, which he loved because it had a great subway system.)

I didn't need my son to fulfill my dreams for me. I wanted him to fulfill his own dreams. He thought that majoring in subways was an odd idea, but as a college professor, I knew it would be possible to do this in one way or another. However, this is not the point of my story.

My son is now grown and works in Washington, D.C., as the head of a transportation policy organization. He recently called me to discuss a choice of two jobs he has been offered. Many people with serious knowledge of his field have offered their advice and counsel. The problem is that people assume they know who my son is and what he wants. I know that his real question is which of these jobs is on the path to running a subway system. Understanding the *real question* is the most important step in making decisions. The real question for students is what they want in life. No one can tell them the answer, but we can help them to seek and find those answers.

To prove this point, ask a few young people to list five objectives or goals they want to achieve. Then ask if they really understand these goals. You can't say you want to be a lawyer if you don't know what lawyers actually do. You must spend some time in a legal office to find out. I wonder why it isn't the school's job to take all of those aspiring lawyers and give them a dose of lawyering? This would be difficult to do, however, given the amount of officially mandated curriculum schools need to cover.

Next, ask these young people to list the goal or goals their parents want them to achieve. Then have them make a specific argument as to why their parents might be wrong. Their parents do not have to be wrong; they may be right. However, one needs to think about the other side of any issue in order to really understand it. The point here is to help children know how to justify their choices in life beyond just mindlessly following an expected path. Schools don't try to help students set goals, and therein lies the biggest mistake that schools make.

Setting Goals for School

Simply put, students should be allowed to choose what they want to learn in school. No one is good at everything. While I was a professor at Yale, I helped with graduate admissions. If I saw a college transcript with all A's, I wondered what that student was really like. What did he or she really know and like to do, or was he or she just trying to be good at school? Is it better to be really good at something than mindlessly good at everything? I didn't want graduate students whose main passion was pleasing the teacher.

We must understand, in this context, that the goals schools set for students don't actually make a lot of sense. School can tell you that algebra or history is important, but students might ask, "Important for what?" If a student has no real interest in a subject, he or she can study hard, but in the long run, it doesn't really work. Students won't remember most of what they learned in a few years (or even a few weeks). So, why bother?

Let's start by asking about the goals children actually have. Children have career goals, in part, because they are asked all the time by adults what they want to be when they grow up.

In 2012, the U.S. Bureau of Labor Statistics polled several hundred children, between the ages of five and twelve, who live in and around New York City. Following are the top ten career aspirations the children claimed to have, in order of most desired to least desired (Doyle, n.d.).

1. Astronaut
2. Musician
3. Actor
4. Dancer
5. Teacher
6. Firefighter
7. Police officer
8. Writer
9. Detective
10. Athlete

What can we make of this? Two questions arise from these data: How do children happen to get these goals? What can we learn about how school might change as a result of this information?

How Children Get These Goals

In addressing the first question, it's clear enough how children get these goals. Children learn about these professions by seeing them regularly on television or in the movies and, in part, because they understand these professions. They see athletes on television, and they can play some kind of sport. They see actors, dancers, and detectives on television too, and they get an idea about what these jobs might be like. Children take ballet lessons, act in class plays, and take class trips to the local fire station.

This is all a bit ironic. While school does not purport to teach anything about careers, instead focusing on academic subjects, it actually spends a great deal of time talking about professions children might eventually pursue. It just does it in an odd way.

My grandson wanted to be a teacher for a while because teachers tell students what to do, and he likes telling people what to do. The school encourages involvement in class plays and teaches music. Suddenly, he wanted to be an actor. The school also teaches mathematics, but most students typically don't want to be mathematicians because they have no idea what that job might entail.

Am I suggesting that schools teach students about the jobs that are out there and help them find out which of those jobs is interesting to them? Yes, I am proposing exactly that.

Schools already teach students about professional goals and careers, but they teach them in a random and haphazard way. When a class takes a field trip to the local fire station, the goal is not to promote firefighting as a career choice, but that is exactly what happens. When a school puts on a play, it's promoting the idea of becoming an actor, which is continuously reinforced by movies and television. The schools are indeed promoting professional goals and careers without realizing it.

How School Might Change as a Result

The second question is how school might change as a result of this information. Currently, schools do not provide an individualized curriculum; students have no choices. When I was a child, if I was given the choice of going to a ball game, a concert, or a play, I would have chosen a ball game every time. This choice might not have helped me make career choices, but it would have helped my teachers understand what motivated me. As long as we prevent children from making choices, we won't find out about their real goals. Had my teachers known I wanted to be a baseball player, it wouldn't really have mattered very much because I didn't have the talent. However, my teachers never asked what I wanted to be, and I just kept looking at what was easiest of all the subjects they taught, which for me was mathematics. They didn't teach anything about business, for example, which would have been worth knowing (at least for me).

In today's world, we may not really want to discover who each child is or the goals children might have, but we can help them learn more about their goals. Instead, we decide for children and then push our own goals on them. But does the current curriculum even reflect our goals? It seems to reflect Harvard's goals, but no current faculty at Harvard has been consulted about this; and if it was, nothing would change anyway. It is all set in stone.

Occasionally, there is a push for change. At the writing of this book, the buzzword is *STEM* (science, technology, engineering, and mathematics). Suddenly, everyone needs to study more science (and, of course, more mathematics). Why? I have no idea. I am sure someone is making money in this, but it isn't as if there aren't lots of unemployed physics majors.

The National STEM Centre (2012) commissioned a survey of one thousand children ages six through sixteen. The study reveals that seven of the top ten children's dream jobs are in STEM. However, almost 50 percent of children think the subjects are too difficult or boring to study, posing a huge barrier to achievement. The top ten dream jobs are as follows.

1. Professional athlete
2. Performer
3. Secret agent
4. Firefighter
5. Astronaut
6. Veterinarian
7. Doctor
8. Teacher
9. Pilot
10. Zookeeper

Zookeeper? Really? The people who push STEM pretty much claim anything as STEM. STEM is actually the old 1892 curriculum in new clothing. Finding engineering courses in high school is still difficult. And while most schools have some version of a computer-programming course, they don't offer much more. The STEM push still doesn't change the fact that Harvard decided what students study in high school, which means students are taking all the usual subjects. History, literature, and foreign language are all still there; engineering is not.

However, it is exciting that children seem to want STEM careers, isn't it? By any reasonable measure, though, very few of the careers listed can be seen as STEM careers, and this list looks a lot like the previous list from the U.S. Bureau of Labor Statistics (Doyle, n.d.).

Most of this report is meaningless except for one key statement: ". . . almost half of children (49.4 percent) think that STEM subjects are too difficult or boring to study, posing a huge barrier to them achieving their dream career" (National STEM Centre, 2012). Is this true? You can't be a zookeeper if you don't study algebra? Why not? One possible reason is because Harvard won't accept you if you don't take algebra, although I'm not sure how many Harvard-educated zookeepers there are. But the more important issue is that students think STEM subjects are boring. I wonder why? Maybe . . . because they are. They also are irrelevant. Doctors don't need to know algebra, nor do secret agents.

Something is really wrong here. We bore students with subjects we say they must learn in order to get jobs while being completely uninterested in the fact that those subjects would not help them get those jobs in any way. What we mean is that the schools have established a set of arbitrary requirements that say you can't be a doctor if you don't study algebra and never ask why we think one is related to the other.

How We Can Change School

Here is my radical idea. Allow students who want to be doctors to learn what it's like to be a doctor. They should practice diagnosis, meet fictional patients and prescribe courses of treatment, and otherwise role-play doctoring in real ways. Then, if students really need to know something to play this role (such as how chemicals work in the body and the effects of the drugs they prescribe), we could teach them that instead of teaching them how to balance chemical equations or making them memorize phyla names.

Accomplishing this would require two simple tasks: find out the actual goals students have, and let students experiment in those areas while they are young (as well as suggest enticing goals they may not have considered). We could then teach subjects in context, if these subjects are actually needed to accomplish the goals students have identified.

If, after experimenting with a certain goal, students decide they don't like it after all, we could let them experiment with something else. Because students don't really know what their goals are, we could build on their interests and make school meaningful—and fun!

Let's consider the top professions of interest to children, according to the Bureau of Labor Statistics in 2012 (Doyle, n.d.). I suggest eliminating everything we teach in school today (except reading, writing, and basic mathematics). Instead, let's substitute the desired career curriculum.

At the beginning of the school year, ask every third-grade student to choose one of these careers or any other career that didn't make the list. Then focus on involving that student in the tasks and activities associated with that career. If possible, provide real experiences; if not, provide simulated experiences if that's the best alternative. This is the critical part. Let's take three of these examples: firefighter, actor, and detective.

Imagine the firefighting curriculum. Students would participate in a simulation in which they play the role of trainees in a fire department. It would look a lot like a video game, except without competition. Students would work together to put out fires and choose from a variety of methods to do it. We would not teach them about hoses, water, oxygen, or death by smoke inhalation. Instead, we would start with simple situations, but the tasks would not be so easy. Students would fail. The teacher would discuss what happened, and then students would try again. In order to be good at their jobs, students would need to learn teamwork, communication, and how to write reports. After some time, they would be required to figure out how to improve firefighting by finding new solutions to complex problems. These could be problems with equipment design, building design, human error, flammable materials improperly used or stored, and more.

My point is simple: students can learn nearly any subject through firefighting. History? Some buildings are older, and building materials were different in 1750, 1850, and 1950. Knowing how to identify each material, why it looks the way it does, what it is made of, and how to deal with it in a firefighting situation is a lesson in history. Literature? Why not have students read and write about fires and firefighting?

Students can learn about nearly anything by concentrating on a subject they love. Why can't we let students who want to be firefighters study firefighting in as many ways as possible? Imagine how much they would love going to school. There is nothing difficult about what I am proposing. It just requires building a curriculum and letting students opt out when they change their minds.

It also requires something much more clever. There is a lot in my fictional firefighting curriculum that could easily lead one to be a scientist, an engineer, an inventor, a human resources specialist, or an entrepreneur. If a student realized that firefighters need something they don't have, he or she might be encouraged to move into an entrepreneurship curriculum in order to invent and market the item.

Imagine the acting curriculum. Potential actors would have to think and talk about why people feel the way they do and how people behave in real life. Students might be encouraged to improve on a play in which they are acting. They would certainly need to read many plays and learn the history behind them. For example, Shakespeare's *Romeo and Juliet* is difficult to understand without knowing something about history, Italy, and Shakespeare. Students could try acting but also consider careers as writers, psychologists, sociologists, or analysts of the history of theatre.

The detective curriculum would start with cases that were simple to solve and move on to more complex ones. Students would need to learn forensics and DNA analysis. They would learn about bullet trajectories, angles, and basic geometry. They would need to understand why crime occurs and how to prevent it. They also would need to know about poverty and greed and how the world works. They might not become detectives, but they might become interested in pursuing careers as civic officials, activists, or forensic scientists.

The list is endless. Let's engage children in school by letting them have some fun. Let's take the best minds in the country and have them design curricula around students' interests. As long as students are learning to think, the subject doesn't matter. What matters is the ability to reason from evidence.

The National STEM Centre (2012) curriculum list includes the job of zookeeper. I wonder why some children listed zookeeper as a career goal? Could it be because they visited a zoo? Maybe students could help out in a real zoo. Running a zoo presents a complex management situation. It also requires knowledge about food and shelter, the lives and care of wild animals, and the effects of captivity. A zookeeper needs to know about the physiology of animals, the reasons why animals are different from each other, and much more. Would the zookeeper curriculum be effective because it taught STEM? Or, would it be effective because it encouraged students to learn more about science, management, business, and communication? These are the requirements for running a successful (virtual) zoo.

This is all possible to do. We just have to try. Let's start thinking about how. Where do we start? We must start in high school. That is where we lose students. The intellectual experience is so irrelevant that we turn them off to thinking hard and instead, refocus their thoughts on popularity, proms, and football.

Chapter 2
High School: How It Got That Way

It was only high school after all, definitely one of the most bizarre periods in a person's life. How anyone can come through that time well adjusted on any level is an absolute miracle.

—E. A. Bucchianeri, *Brushstrokes of a Gadfly*

It's challenging to even begin thinking about creating something new unless you spend time considering what was there before and why it was created in the first place. In 1892, President Charles Eliot of Harvard, together with a team of other influential people and professors, created today's high school curriculum. They went under the name of *Committee of Ten*.

In the summer of that year, the Committee decided to hold a conference on each subject to determine how long it should be studied in high school and whether these subjects should be required for college admission. The Committee arranged for nine conferences, each devoted to a particular discipline. In each conference, a group of professors for the featured discipline decided that their subject was critical for study in high school. In most cases, they decided that their subject was critical in elementary school as well.

In light of the fact that today's high school students study more or less exactly what was decided for them in 1892, let's consider these decisions and whether they make sense in today's world. Before we begin, it's important to know what Harvard was like at that time. Following is Harvard's 1892 elementary studies list.

- English
- Greek
- Latin
- German
- French
- Ancient history
- Modern history
- Algebra
- Plane geometry
- Physical science (descriptive)
- Physical science (experimental)

Following is Harvard's 1892 advanced studies list.

- Greek
- Latin
- Greek composition
- Latin composition
- German
- French
- Logarithms and trigonometry
- Solid geometry
- Analytic geometry
- Mechanics or advanced algebra
- Physics
- Chemistry

The combination of these subjects is more or less the high school curriculum today. Students today are preparing for Harvard, whether they intend to attend Harvard or not. However, they are preparing for Harvard in 1892. Today, Harvard offers its students hundreds of choices.

Now, let's discuss some of the subjects students take in high school today, one by one.

Chemistry

This subject is a complete waste of time. No high school student should be forced to study chemistry. Do most adults know the elements of the periodic table? Most of us have memorized the formula for salt, but why? Do adults balance chemical equations at any time in their life outside of high school? Do chemists even do this? Most of the people who take chemistry in college intend to be doctors or pharmacists. They are required to take this subject because it is a big part of the test they take to get into medical school. They will, of course, forget what they learned for the most part. However, a doctor should know some chemistry. Doctors might want to know how the drugs they prescribe actually work in the body, for example, but that is not the chemistry they learn in high school or college.

So, why are all students required to study chemistry? The report from the Committee of Ten required it.

This might be simple to explain. Professors know their subjects, and they work on those subjects all day, every day. If you asked them if their subjects are important, they would say *yes*, and they might further say that you were uneducated if you didn't know something about these subjects. Therefore, students study chemistry because in 1892, chemistry professors were on a committee that decided they should.

Students don't study philosophy in high school because that was not a subject at Harvard in 1892, which is a little odd since this subject has been around for a very long time. Students don't study psychology in high school because the subject was not considered very serious in 1892. Students don't study engineering because Harvard didn't have an engineering school, and they don't study business for the same reason. (One would think this state of affairs could be rectified. Harvard has a pretty good business school today. Where is President Eliot when we need him?)

It is a fair question to ask if studying chemistry is in any way relevant for the average person. My answer is *yes*. But this *yes* comes with a different point of view. Let's consider one of the curricula we discussed in chapter 1: firefighting. Is chemistry relevant to the firefighting curriculum? Of course it is. Chemical interactions cause fires and also serve to put out fires. Firefighters need to know a lot about chemicals. But do they need to memorize the elements of the periodic table? Do they need to balance chemical equations? They must learn relevant chemistry as it applies to their job.

In the video-game simulations that I propose, all students would begin their fictional firefighter careers with a range of problems to solve. Some of these would involve chemical issues. Students should have to study and understand these issues as they apply to their fictional job. Our budding firefighters should learn to *reason* about chemistry rather than memorize irrelevant facts and formulas. If students preparing to be firefighters become interested in the chemical reactions they witness in the simulation, they could switch to another curriculum and learn the more technical aspects of chemistry, perhaps even moving into the chemist curriculum. However, forcing the same material down every student's throat, regardless of his or her interests and ambitions, is simply absurd.

Just to be clear what that material consists of, following is a chemistry question from the SAT (The College Board, 2015a).

A type of ion found in aluminum oxide:

A.	X^+	D.	XO_3^{2-}
B.	X^{2+}	E.	XO_4^{2}
C.	X^{3+}		

I took college chemistry for two years. I couldn't even begin to try to answer this question, in part because I simply don't care. And I might add, I could have studied college chemistry without having taken high school chemistry easily enough. It is an illusion that students need this for college.

History

Most of us have heard the old adage that those who don't remember history are doomed to repeat it. However, another adage claims that history is written by the victors. Most of what we learn in history is what we would like to believe. We still hear the ideas that Columbus discovered America and that George Washington never told a lie. Not true but interesting nonetheless.

The real problem in teaching history is that there is a political battle about what history to teach. Studying history has always been a way of indoctrinating students into whatever political opinions those in power happen to hold. In 2014, the Texas State School Board decided to rewrite history once again. They were concerned about the proper amount of emphasis on the Bible in texts used to study the American Revolution. History (at least in Texas) seems to change with each election.

Let's return to the Committee of Ten's opinion on history in 1892. The history faculty of the Committee of Ten felt it had to explain why students needed to study history. They claimed it was for training one's judgment. Funny how that turned into memorizing dates, places of famous battles, and learning about Moses (at least in Texas).

There is, however, plenty of room in the zookeeper curriculum to learn about history. Students could learn where animals come from, who captured them, and under what circumstances. Students also could study what zoos were like in the past and how they have changed over the years, considering ideas of extinction and preservation.

The acting curriculum would require learning enough history to perform a period piece well. And again, as long as we make it interesting and relevant to students' stated goals, students will learn it. If they want to pursue it further, students could then enter the history curriculum. I don't know what jobs they would be prepared for with that curriculum, but I am all for the ability to choose. History should be a choice too, just not a requirement.

Note the following history question from the SAT (The College Board, 2015b).

> The encomienda system of colonial Spanish America most closely resembled the European practice of:
>
> A.　absolutism
>
> B.　primogeniture
>
> C.　patronage
>
> D.　manorialism
>
> E.　nepotism

In case you forgot, questions like these are what studying history in high school is really all about—the all-important "getting into college" test. Do you know the answer to this question? Does it matter if you do? Would you do poorly in college if you didn't?

English

In a choice-based curriculum, students would be encouraged to read books and write about their ideas. Learning to express oneself is very important, but no one ever learns how to do that by writing about a book he or she doesn't enjoy or find interesting.

Why do we require students to study English for four years in high school? We do this because that is what the 1892 report says to do. This idea is usually so ingrained that we don't question it. Some may emphasize that students must learn how to write, think critically, analyze, and use grammar and vocabulary properly. While all of these skills are admirable, they need not be learned as subjects in and of themselves and for four solid years. We can learn to read and write and argue in any context. If students are interested in the context, they are much more likely to remember what they've learned.

Biology

Now here is a subject worth knowing about, but schools don't teach anything that matters. Plant phyla? Amoebas? How about studying the health and care of your own body? Instead, that is relegated to health class.

Following is a biology question from the SAT (The College Board, 2015c).

Nitrogenous base that occurs in RNA but not in DNA:

A. deoxyribose   D. cytosine

B. ribose   E. thymine

C. uracil

Really? Who cares? And why are we cutting up frogs? I took tenth-grade biology, and I don't remember a thing. I wonder if Charles Eliot could have answered this question.

Physics

Physics is another odd subject that students are required to study in high school. The formulas students learn in high school physics are of no use to them. Students study physics so they can answer questions like the following and get into Harvard, where they are likely never to see physics again (The College Board, 2015d).

Which of the following is true of the magnetic field produced by a current in a long, straight wire?

A. The field is uniform.

B. The field increases in strength as the distance from the wire increases.

C.   The field lines are directed parallel to the wire but opposite to the direction of the current.

D.   The field lines are directed radially outward from the wire.

E.   The field lines form circles about the wire.

Of course, the firefighter, the detective, and many other people who work with physical material would need to learn physics, just not the physics taught in high school. Furthermore, physics, like the other subjects discussed, should not be a subject unto itself.

Foreign Language

Universities require foreign languages because, once upon a time, scholars had to read scholarly articles in French or German. Not anymore, as these are all in English today. We could teach students how to speak a foreign language, but we should emphasize speaking and not reading. We could ignore teaching grammar rules too. It also helps to start children when they are very young rather than requiring it in high school. Our unconscious knows how to form a proper sentence and how to understand sentences we hear. This may entail knowing grammar, but it is the kind of knowing that is really *doing*.

I moved to France as an adult armed with three years of high school French. I had learned to say, "Comment allez-vous?" But the French say, "Ça va?" I learned to order *un verre de rouge* to get a glass of red wine in a café. The word *wine* never comes up. We learn a language by trying to communicate in that language. Immersion is the only way. The sooner immersion starts, the better. Interestingly, the Committee of Ten (1892) didn't get this one entirely wrong.

4. OTHER MODERN LANGUAGES.

The most novel and striking recommendation made by the conference on modern languages is that an elective course in German or French be provided in the grammar school, the instruction to be open to children at about 10 years of age. (pp. 1425–1426)

Remember that these are their words, not mine. Funny that the only right-minded recommendation made by this committee was more or less ignored. Some United States schools offer foreign language instruction in the early grades, but most do not. In other countries, they start teaching English as soon as possible. They actually want their students to speak English in the Netherlands and Sweden, so they start in first grade.

Mathematics

And now, we come to my favorite subject—mathematics. This is how the Committee of Ten (1892) viewed mathematics.

5. MATHEMATICS.

The conference recommend that the study of systematic algebra should be begun at the age of fourteen; but that, in connection with the study of arithmetic, the pupils should earlier be made familiar with algebraic expressions and symbols, including the method of solving simple equations. The conference believe that the study of demonstrative geometry should begin at the end of the first year's study of algebra, and be carried on by the side of algebra for the next two years, occupying about two hours and a half a week. (pp. 1426–1427)

And there you have it. Why do we teach ninth graders algebra, followed by geometry, followed by more algebra? Because that is what this committee decided in 1892.

My opinion about studying mathematics is very simple. Don't. Learn the mathematics you need when you need it. Learn the mathematics you need to build a bridge if you are in the bridge-building curriculum, and learn the mathematics you need to properly measure food if you are in the zookeeper curriculum. After the basics in fourth grade, for example, you will never use mathematics again unless you practice it, and you won't practice it unless you really need it.

Considering the Alternatives

Once one has rejected the idea that a group of professors' curricula from 1892 might be at all relevant today, we must ask why education leaders haven't considered alternatives. The Committee of Ten decided that even students who were not planning to attend college should study the subjects they recommended. This decision has had profound implications for anybody going to school after 1892 until the present day.

Is there something sacrosanct about what subjects happened to be taught at Harvard in 1892? Are they somehow more important than other subjects because they were there first? University departments are self-perpetuating. Faculties survive at all costs. At the writing of this book, humanities faculties are under attack. Some faculties defend themselves by claiming that students can't learn to reason without studying the humanities. Peter Burian (2012) writes, "Long gone are the days when academic humanists could sit like dragons astride their hoards of high culture. Today, we have become contrarians, for better or worse, battling adversity from without and uncertainty within. And yet, what we have to offer is needed now more than ever." The humanities are under attack because their professors can't find jobs. Today's students are more interested in technology and business than they are in literature. Universities will adapt. High schools can't.

The subjects from 1892 are still around, but the more contemporary subjects might just be more relevant in the 21st century. Following are a few subjects currently taught at Harvard that might be better, and certainly more interesting, to study in high school than those schools actually teach.

- Anthropology
- Astronomy
- Business studies
- Computer science
- Engineering sciences
- Environmental science and public policy
- Government
- Health policy
- Medical sciences
- Mind, brain, and behavior
- Oceanography
- Philosophy
- Psychology
- Public policy
- Social policy
- Statistics

However, this is not what I'm suggesting. The educated mind is not created by the study of all the subjects that happened to be at Harvard in 1892, nor is it likely to be created by studying those at Harvard today. College preparation should not be the sole purpose of K–12 education. This made little enough sense when it was unlikely that the average high school student went to college. It makes even less sense when we realize that colleges can teach whatever subjects they want while leaving high schools alone.

Harvard should not be in the position to determine what K–12 education should look like. We must define what it means for 21st century high school graduates to be properly educated. We must create a high school experience in which students learn skills that enhance their daily lives and open up their minds to every possibility, not just prepare them for college.

Let the colleges teach whatever they want to teach, but we must stop them from dictating what high schools teach.

Chapter 3
New Curricula for a New Era

According to my view, anyone who would be good at anything must practice that thing from his youth upwards.

—Plato

So, what can we build to replace what was handed down to us by Eliot and his cohorts and modified to make "plug-compatible" children by Bill Gates and the Common Core?

We have what we need to build the education system of the future. It includes realistic simulations, online mentoring, real choices, and students working together to solve problems with the help of experts. Because of advanced technology tools, these experts can be physically present as well as virtually connected around the world.

Ten Criteria for the New Curricula

Any new curriculum must have the following ten criteria.

1. Learning by doing
2. Student choice for learning

3. Meaningful projects with clear goals

4. Regular, realistic deliverables

5. Designed around a profession

6. Delivered on the web

7. Mentored by teachers, experts, and parents

8. Designed by world-class experts

9. Collaborative teams

10. Communication, reasoning, and human relations

Let's consider these one at a time.

Learning by Doing

Students learn by doing; curricula consist of a series of projects inside a coherent story about life in some aspect of the real world.

Why is this important? Because, as Plato said, this is how we actually learn. We learn to drive a car by driving, not by reading the manual. We learn to hit a baseball by swinging a bat. We learn to write by writing, speak by speaking, program a computer by programming, and make money by acquiring a valuable skill.

Student Choice for Learning

Choice must be a staple. Students select the curricula in which they wish to participate.

This is important because children have choices as they grow up. They select which games and toys interest them, which places outside the house they want to go, and who they want to play with. Then suddenly, without warning, all choice is taken away. They must sit still and pay attention to what the teacher is saying and learn various facts to be tested on. They don't get to choose, and they don't get to actually do much of anything. They do get to take tests—lots of them. Testing comprises much of the doing students do. Students are being trained to be test takers. How much sense does this make?

No matter how many times teachers tried to teach me about music or art, I didn't care. I tuned it all out. Would I have been better off if I had paid attention? I don't think so. I paid attention to what interested me. I liked mathematics. I thought about mathematics when no one made me do it. In college, I discovered that mathematics was too abstract for me. Instead, I started thinking about computers. I made my choices by tuning out what I didn't like. As a result, I was a C student and had trouble getting into my preferred colleges. The earlier a student gets to choose, the less likely he or she is to tune out. Students who are passionate about what they are doing stay in school, and they keep learning. Forcing students to study subjects they don't care about achieves nothing.

Meaningful Projects With Clear Goals

Curricula must be designed around projects with clear, meaningful, and achievable goals. To say that learning involves meaningful goals would seem perfectly obvious if it weren't for the fact that schools simply don't follow this rule. People typically don't learn something because they have to; they learn it because they truly want to (or they don't learn it very well). Usually, they are trying to acquire a skill, whether it is persuading people to buy something, building something, or learning how something works. A meaningful goal is always behind it. When you hear ordinary people talk about issues in their lives, these issues typically involve money, work, family, or relationships. Their goals naturally come from these issues. Schools must address the goals that people actually have, not the ones that Charles Eliot wanted them to have.

NEW YORK INSTITUTE
OF TECHNOLOGY

Regular, Realistic Deliverables

Students must submit deliverables related to each project for evaluation and feedback. There are no tests of inert knowledge, only performance tests.

Why does this matter? Today's school system is obsessed with tests. The reason for this is probably commercial. A great deal of money is made through testing. Texas spends $468 million a year to grade the tests administered in that state (Weiss, 2015). And that is just one state!

Are these tests valid in any way? Preparing for these tests, which has become the obsession of teachers and principals everywhere, is certainly a good way to do better on other tests. So, if we accept that tests actually test something worth knowing, then the more testing there is, the more students will achieve better test scores. But why does this matter?

It matters to the people who make money on testing. And it tends to matter to politicians who can say they improved test scores. Does it matter to the students? In the first class I taught each year at Yale and Northwestern, I would ask my students if they could pass the tests they took the previous year. Most agreed that they could not. But, they said, if they studied they could pass.

What have we created? We have created a system in which students know how to cram information in order to pass a test. But the subject matter of those tests typically never comes up in students' lives after the course, so, naturally they forget what they "learned."

The only valid tests are performance tests. However, the tests we use in schools are meant to be easy to grade, so we don't test items that are subjective or involve doing. When I visit a doctor, I don't care if he or she did well on the bone name memorization test in medical school. I care about how many cases just like mine he or she has treated in his or her career.

We must be sure that students are asked to perform and that teachers are good judges of what excellent performance looks like. Students learn to be expert performers through constant, mentored practice.

Designed Around a Profession

Curricula focus on actual professions, not academic subjects. As a society, we decided that intellectual subjects are the natural domains of schools. As a result, we teach what professors study, quite literally. One might ask why this is the case. The answer is that if you are going to attend Harvard and study mathematics or literature, Harvard professors don't want to have to teach the basics to every entering student. Harvard accepts students who have shown some capability in these areas. This is a rational point of view if you are at Harvard.

In high school, everyone is preparing for college, which means they are studying intellectual subjects. Does this make sense? Our society isn't deficient in intellectuals. All societies need people to do the jobs that are available or to help create new jobs. There aren't that many openings for historians. If high schools prepared students for real life rather than college, they would not teach subjects; and if they did, these subjects wouldn't be the same as those taught at Harvard in 1892.

Delivered on the Web

The new curricula must be delivered on the web. Students submit their work to mentors and receive feedback online.

Why must the curricula of the future be delivered online? We are all used to school being a place where one is physically present. This makes sense in a world where everyone is studying the same subjects. But in order to allow a student who is interested in becoming a doctor to study medicine or a student who wants to be an aerospace engineer to study engineering, we would require more specialized teachers in the school building than is actually possible.

It is impossible for a child's every conceivable interest to be covered by teachers who are physically present. We must find another way.

Schools, after all, have as their primary (and often unstated) purpose—day care. Schools make sure that children aren't wandering the streets unsupervised and enable parents to work. In an era in which both parents are often working, this is becoming even more important. Simply putting curricula online and having students do their work whenever and wherever is probably an unlikely and undesirable outcome. Schools may well continue as day-care centers, but that doesn't mean they have to teach in the same way that they have always taught.

Online curricula currently have a relatively unsavory reputation. This is due to the fact that most people building online curricula are trying to teach what always has been taught in the way it always has been taught. Therefore, textbooks, quizzes, and lectures find their way online in a form that is even worse than that of a traditional classroom. People have become naturally prejudiced against this.

Consider a flight simulator, for example. Many pilots learn to fly by flying a simulated airplane. The United States Department of Defense felt that this was the best way to train pilots, and it spent the money to build flight simulators.

Why wouldn't a doctor simulator be the best way to train doctors, a courtroom simulator be the best way to train lawyers, or a construction site simulator be the best way to train construction site managers? Any real skill can be taught by simulation if the money is available to build high-quality simulators in which students can start simply, practice, and take on progressively more difficult tasks.

What is missing from this scenario is the teacher. Am I proposing that students work alone in a simulator without teachers? No, absolutely not. Flight simulators were built decades ago when the web didn't exist and online communication didn't exist. Today, a teacher (actually, a mentor, or a teacher who is there to help rather than instruct) could be available to answer questions and give helpful suggestions as students progress through a simulation.

Teachers would still be needed to help frustrated students, offer new choices, assist with team conflicts, offer friendly advice, and maintain student safety. Teachers could also be mentors while students are attempting more traditional tasks, but they may not be capable if students are designing a 787 airliner. In that case, specialized expertise is available, but the expert may be in another state or even another country. Online delivery allows that kind of mentoring to happen.

Mentored by Teachers, Experts, and Parents

Mentoring must be about helping students think through a problem without giving them the answer. Why is this important? Not only is the subject matter in question but also traditional teaching methods. People don't learn just by listening, and they certainly don't learn through temporary memorization. Teachers teach incorrectly, but it's not their fault. Good teaching is one-on-one teaching. Parents don't try to raise thirty children at once, nor do they teach their children at prescribed times with prepared lessons. Children learn from their parents in a natural way through conversation and observation. In the schools I am envisioning, teachers would have the time to engage in meaningful dialogue with students when students need the support of mentors.

A teacher's role also would include listening to student presentations about their work and reading their reports on a regular basis. Students would learn to speak, write, and reason clearly, skills that apply to every kind of job in the real world. A former classroom teacher could teach all of these skills in his or her new mentoring role.

Designed by World-Class Experts

The new curricula must be designed by world-class experts from top universities and specific fields and industries. A pilot who also manufactured keyboard organs designed the first widely used flight simulator. An airline manufacturer designed the second most widely used flight simulator after World War II (Fly Away Simulation, 2010). What does this mean? While education professionals would be helpful in designing new curricula, the critical players are practitioners in a given field or industry—for example, those who know what real courtrooms feel like and what happens in them, those who have started businesses and understand the issues involved, and those who have designed cities and understand urban design. Curricula designers must understand that making the student experience realistic and authentic is of utmost importance. The pedagogical issues revolve around capturing the students' attention and putting students in situations that demand complex reasoning and explanation. The real purpose of any of these curricula is to require analytical thinking and decision making and acquire expertise in the service of achieving a desired goal.

This only can be done in consultation with experts who can tell designers what kinds of decisions, behaviors, or achievements must be made in a given field, and can put students into situations where they might make the wrong decision, do the wrong thing, or attempt to build something and build it badly. The student, with the help of mentors, then has to figure out what went awry and determine how to fix it.

Collaborative Teams

In the new curricula, students are encouraged to work in teams (virtual or live), learning to collaborate with others in order to produce results.

Why should students work in teams? The first reason is because working on a computer is a very isolating experience. If that's what a student does all day, the simulation really won't work. But an equally important reason is that when we think about what is important to learn, working with and getting along with others must be a very high priority. Communicating and collaborating with others is a high priority in life. Adults work in teams in nearly every job situation. Why these skills are overlooked in schools makes no sense. (When students actually do this, it's called *cheating*.)

Communication, Reasoning, and Human Relations

The overarching theme of a particular curriculum is not the most important goal for learning. In the end, students might want to become firefighters, zookeepers, doctors, or lawyers. They should have the opportunity to practice skills associated with these careers to find out if they like them. However, some skills are more important to learn than the particulars of being a firefighter or a doctor. Students must learn to solve problems and negotiate issues for themselves. They must learn to diagnose situations, make judgments, and create effective plans. They must know how to try out new situations to discover if they are working. They need to be able to convince people of their point of view. Students must learn each of these skills no matter what career they choose. Therefore, while each curriculum would focus on a professional skill of interest, it would also incorporate other skills and tasks that may well be more important. Each curriculum must be structured so that thinking, communicating, collaborating, and getting along with others dominate each day's work.

Five Types of Curricular Experiences

The previous ten criteria represent a point of view on what well-designed curricula should look like. Now, let's be a bit more specific.

We can build five types of mentored curricular experiences: (1) mentored simulations, (2) real-life experiences, (3) stand-alone simulations, (4) online collaborative activities, and (5) learning-by-doing experiences. There might be more, but we don't want every curriculum we build to look the same. The reason is simple: curricula are designed differently because the learning is different and requires varied methodologies. Following are descriptions of five types of curricular experiences, along with some examples.

Mentored Simulations

Sometimes it's a good idea to establish an elaborate fiction within which students can play roles. The reason for this is simple enough. If you want to run a business, the best way to learn how to do that would be to run an actual business. Another way would be to help someone run a business and learn what needs to be done through that mentor. My mother ran a business, which was started by her father. Throughout my childhood, she was his second in command. Eventually, he was too elderly to run it, so she took over. The business did better than ever. She had plenty of time to learn how to run it. She took more control with every passing year. Of course she knew how to run the business.

Reality works as an educational experience. School is, in a sense, an attempt to shortcut reality. My mother spent maybe thirty years learning to run that business. Had she gone to school and learned about business (my mother never graduated high school), she probably wouldn't have learned much that would have helped her run her particular business.

However, practice with running a fictional business might have helped. Why? When you're in school, you can make mistakes that don't cost anything. You can always start over and try again. In a well-designed mentored simulation, people are around to help when needed, both live mentors and experts who have been recruited, interviewed on video, and placed in the simulation at appropriate points. These experts would be consulted to help design fictional situations that pose exactly the kinds of challenges one only experiences in that field, even rare situations.

Practicing a situation that rarely occurs is difficult, but in a fictional simulation, anything can happen. Preparing for the worst can be easily accomplished in a simulation by designing situations in which the worst happens. Of course, it is best to start with simple situations and then proceed to more complex ones. However, real life doesn't typically work like that. Real life happens as it happens and is not designed for learning simple skills that we can build on in the next situation. But this is exactly how a mentored simulation should work if it is designed properly.

In these work simulations, students would play a role in which they would be required to produce documents, software, plans, presentations, and so on, within those fictional simulations. Team members and mentors would then evaluate student deliverables.

Real-Life Experiences

Real life is a good teacher. It always has been. For some reason, as a society, we have adopted the idea that sitting in a classroom is the best way to educate children. If they see real life at all in their teenage years, they do it through summer jobs.

When I was sixteen years old, my summer job was working for my mother delivering packages throughout New York City to various businesses in the fashion industry. My mother was a great mom but not a great teacher. She believed I should start at the bottom, so I swept the floor and even hauled garbage. I couldn't wait for the summer to be over. She never tried to teach me about the business, which was odd because she wanted me to take over the business someday. I learned about New York City, though. It was not a great learning experience, but it could have been.

The summer I turned eighteen, I was hired as an actuarial trainee for the Mutual Benefit Life Insurance Company in Newark, New Jersey. I figured this might be a good fit for someone who was skilled at mathematics, so maybe this would be a possible career for me someday. I hated it. I learned that I didn't want to work for a big company and sit in a room with a hundred desks. I learned that being an actuary was boring. And, I learned that jobs actually existed in which all one did was take numbers from a computer, make calculations, and then send new numbers back to the computer. (When I wrote a computer program to eliminate my job, they got mad at me.)

There is a great deal to learn from real experiences. But what I am about to propose is something rather radical. When students are about sixteen years old, allow them to skip school all together and take jobs. These jobs would work similar to the way summer jobs work now in that the main goal is to introduce students to what having a job is really like. The schools, or districts, would be in charge of a very organized system of possible jobs. Students could make better choices, supervision would be established to be sure students were not abused in any way, and most importantly, students would spend part of each week discussing, writing about, and sharing their work experiences with a skilled mentor.

The problem with my two summer jobs is that neither was intended as an educational experience. My mother could have made it more educational if a school official had provided suggestions for what that experience should be like and was intentionally part of my education. Mutual Benefit was not trained in how to provide education. This company was looking for future employees but going about it the wrong way. It too could have offered an educationally oriented program that both taught the student and provided the same test of work capabilities it was seeking in employees.

More specifically, my proposal is this: In cooperation with local companies and businesses, schools excuse students from school to work for a year when they are sixteen. Instead of being concerned with whether we are preparing students for college, this plan prepares them for life. College students who have had real jobs are usually better students when they get to college, at least that was my observation. They know more about the world of work, how to approach and accomplish tasks, and how to collaborate with others. Working not only teaches students about the real world but also allows them to try something new that might be of interest. The work I am suggesting would be supervised, in part, by mentors and used as a way of learning to think about one's experiences. We could help students come to conclusions about how the world actually works and, as a result, produce fewer young people who are unprepared for life after school.

Students might work on a construction site, do clerical work at a law firm, be a nurse's aide in a hospital, apprentice at a software company or in a retail store, help out on a farm or in a restaurant, assist in a veterinary clinic or in an animal shelter, or work at hundreds of other places that would be willing to hire and teach them for one year. At the end of the year, students would be capable of making much better decisions about their lives. We must ensure that students see, experience, and function in the real world.

After my experience at Mutual Benefit, I vowed never to work for a large business again. However, when I was in graduate school, I had no choice but to take a job with a large firm so I could support myself. Again, I hated it. I never did it again. These were great learning experiences for me. I learned about the world, and I learned about myself.

Stand-Alone Simulations

Elaborate computer simulations allow students to have experiences that would otherwise be impossible or dangerous. Computer simulations can be used to teach students how to fly a plane, manage people, or run a political campaign.

We have used these kinds of simulations for many years to teach specific skills. For example, my company, Socratic Arts, was asked by one of the largest firms in the United States to teach sexual harassment policies online. Your first thought might be to build a simulation in which a man and woman interact to demonstrate harassment. But that is just silly. No one is going to harass a fictional person, and setting up such a situation realistically is more or less impossible. Instead, we created a job that none of the students taking the sexual harassment course were actually training for. We taught them how to be sexual harassment judges. Their job was to hear the evidence on both sides in a dispute and make a determination according to the law. In this way, they learned the rules and the company could check off the box that said they provided sexual harassment training. It was fiction, and we weren't really training anyone for anything, but the students liked it and thought about the issues more deeply.

For younger students, many activities and scenarios might work well as simulations. In the mid-1990s, the Institute for the Learning Sciences at Northwestern built a simulation designed for people at the Environmental Protection Agency (EPA) to learn how to run a public meeting. Participants met with fictional stakeholders and tried to run a fictional meeting. They sought help from videotaped EPA experts and learned just how tough it was to actually run a meeting without, for example, a stakeholder getting angry because his or her favorite issue wasn't being handled the way he or she wanted. The lesson of this software was to do your homework, which in this case, meant meeting with every stakeholder individually beforehand so that no surprises would arise at the actual meeting. We made the software simulation fun and realistic, and the EPA uses it to this very day.

Online Collaborative Activities

We can create intellectual experiences for students that require little more than utilizing the power of the web. For example, students in one country could discuss their lives with students living in different societies and cultures. Students could debate issues, work as a group to develop ideas, and attempt collaborative projects. Imagine students in Pakistan working with students in the state of Kansas, trying to understand each other's daily lives and then trying to help their parents understand as well.

For example, students in the United States could make a video about their city or town and show it to students on the other side of the world. Those foreign students could judge whether the videos make sense to them, and then groups could help each other to communicate better about issues in their part of the world. Students could interview their grandparents to learn more about the history of their lives. They could then try to explain what their world is like and why, with some historical context, while learning about themselves at the same time.

Alternatively, students could generate ideas in a specific problematic area and discuss them with experts in that discipline. Imagine, for example, students in a lower socioeconomic part of a community exploring how to reduce crime and getting experts involved in the conversation. Students could work with others in their community to try to reduce conflicts that arise from misunderstandings between ethnic groups or social classes. Projects they might work on could include making a video, producing a song, or finding a common problem in their community and working with others to solve it. Instead of sitting in a classroom reading about ancient history, wouldn't it be more effective if students learned about problems within their own communities?

Learning-by-Doing Experiences

Many children are fascinated with constructing and building objects. This is why LEGOs, erector sets, and blocks have been so popular over the years. For this reason, my nonprofit organization, Engines for Education, built an engineering curriculum meant to occupy a full year of a student's time in the second or third grade. The students work through a series of engineering projects by following a basic engineering process: design, build, test, and revise. This is not done online because it is real and physical. Also, young children need to be active and should not be spending too much time staring at a computer screen.

The projects are designed to help students practice skills such as diagnosing, planning, experimenting, and modeling. While this is an engineering curriculum, we still teach reading, writing, and arithmetic. We also don't ignore teamwork and communication skills. These concepts are all taught in context. Instead of reading about Dick and Jane, students read about earthquakes, airplanes, and bridges.

This curriculum is designed for a teacher working with about six students. Typically, two teams of three try to accomplish each project with the teacher's assistance. These are physical projects; students must build things. We do not expect the teacher to know all there is to know about engineering, so we use extensive supporting material on the web. But in the case of such young students, that material is meant for the teacher, not the children. We want students to learn by doing, and for an eight-year-old, this means *physical doing*.

Maybe some people really like sitting at a desk, listening to the teacher, and answering questions. I know I wasn't one of them. The school called my mother to ask why I was so difficult. My mother told them, "Give him a broom and have him sweep up. He's bored to death. At least that way he would stop having to sit, and he could actually *do* something." She was a wise lady. We should all be so wise.

Chapter 4
Making School Fun

The only thing that interferes with my learning is my education.

—Albert Einstein

When we consider young people who have not succeeded in traditional school settings, we need not ask what is wrong with them but what is wrong with traditional school settings. Many successful people have had great difficulty in traditional school settings.

Albert Einstein (1956), who succeeded well enough in a school like the one Eliot proposed, states:

> The point is to develop the childlike inclination for play and the childlike desire for recognition and to guide the child over to important fields for society . . . Such a school demands from the teacher that he be a kind of artist in his province. (p. 35)

The Change We Need

At least four aspects of school need to change in order to make school fun and relevant to students' lives in the real world.

1. Role of the teacher

2. Emphasis on success rather than failure

3.   Relevance of learning to children's goals

4.   A motivating, story-centered curriculum

Role of the Teacher

Teachers would be great to have around if they were there only when you needed them. Parents, the original teachers of children, are, if the child is lucky, around when needed. This model of education, inherent in being a child, includes involvement in activities of the child's choosing mediated by an adult who can help if the child feels the need for assistance.

It's clear why traditional schools do not operate this way. One cannot expect a teacher to be able to respond effectively to a classroom of forty students, each working on an individual project. Of course, some schools actually try to accomplish this goal, such as Montessori schools. But, even those schools give up on this model of education when faced with curricula that must be taught and tests that must be passed. Class size and curriculum bind the teacher, making him or her a provider of information and judge of correct answers rather than a mentor who is there for support and assistance.

The model of the teacher as midwife is quite ancient, as evidenced in thoughts expressed by Socrates.

> *Soc.* Well, my art of midwifery is in most respects like theirs; but differs, in that I attend men and not women, and I look after their souls when they are in labour, and not after their bodies: and the triumph of my art is in thoroughly examining whether the thought which the mind of the young man brings forth is a false idol or a noble and true birth. And like the midwives, I am barren, and the reproach which is often made against me, that I ask questions of others and have not the wit to answer them myself, is very just—the reason is, that the god compels me to be a midwife, but does not allow me to bring forth. And therefore I am not myself at all wise, nor have I anything to show which is the invention or birth of my own soul, but those who converse with me profit. (as cited in Plato, 1892, p. 203)

Socrates was famous for his Socratic method of teaching. He saw himself as a midwife, bringing birth to new ideas in the minds of his students, the seeds of which he claimed not to have planted.

Socrates's idea—that a teacher's only job is to bring out what students already know by asking good questions—may not be entirely effective. Nevertheless, what clearly is true is that asking good questions is more important than supplying answers. A teacher's job is to help students learn how to collaborate, communicate, and reason. The teacher can best accomplish this by being with students at the right time, encouraging them to think hard about what they are trying to do, as expressed by Henry Louis Mencken in 1949.

> It is the mission of the pedagogue, not to make his pupils think, but to make them think *right*, and the more nearly his own mind pulsates with the great ebbs and flows of popular delusion and emotion, the more admirably he performs his function. He may be an ass, but that is surely no demerit in a man paid to make asses of his customers. (p. 316)

Naturally, it is sometimes true that the teacher knows and the student does not. Two plus two really does equal four. So, teachers can hardly avoid getting into the habit of setting themselves up as authorities and expecting students to learn what they teach. There is only one problem with this: it may not work. However, changing the teacher's role from talking to listening and from teaching to mentoring is essential.

We don't actually need authorities to learn how to think. In many ways, it is better to be wrong and learn that you are wrong through experience or through the frustration of having to defend poorly thought-out ideas. In their current form, teachers may have been a good idea at one time, although I am not so sure of this. It's not the teacher's fault, of course. The role of the teacher has been poorly defined, mostly because of the idea that we must have classrooms. Get rid of classrooms, and teachers could behave differently. School would be a lot more fun if students didn't have to worry about what the teacher thought of them or learning whatever it was the teacher just lectured about.

Emphasis on Success Rather Than Failure

As long as teachers make judgments about students, many students will try to please them. It is simple human nature. At that point, original thinking goes out the window. For students who feel they cannot or do not want to please the teacher, school becomes tedious, and learning becomes quite difficult. When students ask themselves how well they are doing, they are asking the wrong question. Instead, they should be thinking about what they are trying to accomplish and how to go about it. As Cicero states, "The authority of those who teach is often an obstacle to those who want to learn."

This is not really an issue of grades; the problem is deeper than that. Children are constantly asked, "How are you doing in school?" Supposedly, the people asking this question want to know if children who are supposed to be learning actually are learning. It seems to be a fair enough question. But, it is one of the most seriously bothersome and difficult questions that our society asks, and it is a primary reason that students fail to learn.

The question is problematic in a number of ways. The primary problem is with the basic assumption that educational achievement is measurable. As a society, we believe this so strongly that it is very difficult for anyone to suggest that this is the beginning of the problem for students who do not succeed in school. Following on the heels of that issue is how the attempt to measure learning influences what we teach.

This is the real problem with the Common Core. Why do we need all these measures? In recent years, the focus has been on whether teachers are doing their jobs. If stuffing information into a student's head is the real goal, then one can measure a teacher by how much he or she managed to stuff in. However, if inspiring students to get excited about learning is the teacher's goal, how can we measure that?

No one is interested in that kind of measurement. We want numbers that tell us how much mathematics has been retained. Why? Here again, it is to help Harvard with their admissions process.

When we consider the reasons why some students do not do well in traditional school settings, we also must reevaluate what it means to do well. It might mean more than telling teachers (or these days, the testing apparatus, which is way beyond teacher control) the answers they want to hear. Doing well isn't always a good thing. Those who are good at school are good at following the rules and doing what they are told. It is well to remember that our schools were designed to train factory workers.

Relevance of Learning to Children's Goals

In order to transform the education experience for students, we must consider changes in *what* we teach as well as *how* we teach. Every teacher is constrained by a curriculum that a committee somewhere determined must be taught. Students who fail to learn algebra, chemistry, or English literature haven't failed. They have the right to not care about learning these subjects. Students who don't care about the subjects Charles Eliot dictated can still lead happy and productive lives. Perhaps, instead, we might consider giving students more meaningful and personally relevant educational experiences. This is easy to say but difficult to accomplish. There are too many vested interests in what is already in the curricula. Teachers are familiar with it, students expect it, states require it, testing services test it, publishers publish it, and, perhaps most importantly, parents have all experienced it and come to accept it. Schools are armored against change.

The good news is that the Internet can change all of this. Allowing that to happen, however, involves rethinking the notion of what we teach, starting at the very concept of a course. Why do we have courses? The simple answer is that they make life easier for teachers. University professors do not want to spend all day teaching. Why do all courses magically require forty hours of student work? In any course, students should accomplish tasks and, having accomplished them, move on to other tasks. They should have the opportunity to practice and perfect actual skills.

A Motivating, Story-Centered Curriculum

A good curriculum should tell a story, a story in which students play one or more roles. A curriculum should focus on teaching students how to do something. The roles should be ones in which graduates of such a program might actually participate in real-life work environments.

The story-centered curriculum (SCC) is in many ways the antithesis of the idea of putting courses on the web. To put courses on the web, should one simply replicate the existing course content and put that material online? Why would that be a good idea? Is there no more to education than handing out the materials?

To put education online, we must consider the kinds of stories we want students to experience. An SCC can utilize existing teachers and some of the existing materials by having teachers support a story that students actually live. We can build learning-by-doing curricula that require tasks from real-life situations students choose to try.

For example, the story of running a business might include making a business plan, executing that plan, and adjusting the plan for mistaken assumptions. In a story that involves playing a role on a team dealing with particular business issues over a period of time, the teacher (or mentor) would give students tasks within that story to plan and execute the business. Students would work with specified materials to help them execute assigned tasks, and mentors would help them when they had questions or needed guidance. The beauty of this type of scenario is that it can all be done online anytime and anywhere. Students could work in online teams and receive online help from live mentors. Students choose the experience they want and then live and breathe the curriculum they selected, making education relevant to the real world.

What would it mean to build an SCC that worked for young people? It would start with an understanding of the kinds of subjects that interest them. We would need to understand their aspirations, abilities, interests, and fascinations. While a student might not care about learning algebra, he or she might care about building bridges. While a student may not care about writing proper sentences, he or she might want to work in television. While a student may be failing chemistry, he or she may still want to be a health care worker.

To build an SCC, we must ask the following five questions.

1. What short-term or long-term goals do students have? How can we design situations that help students attain skills instrumental to achieving those goals?

2. What does a person who has achieved the goal to which the student aspires actually do all day?

3. What events might occur in the daily life of a person who has achieved such a goal?

4. What story can we construct that plausibly describes a natural sequence of events in the life of a practitioner in a particular field?

5. How can we determine what a student entering a certain curriculum would need to be able to do before starting (that might not necessarily be part of the story)?

It is not actually essential that students know their life goals when selecting an SCC. This is true for three reasons.

1. Many SCCs appropriate for high school students are about living in the adult world. An SCC about hospitals, for example, would engage students with medical issues, financial/business issues, and social

issues. Students need not want to be doctors or nurses to find the hospital SCC compelling, as they will surely use medical services during their lives.

2. When properly constructed, SCCs teach a wide range of skills, such as writing, relevant mathematics, teamwork, planning, and reasoning that transcend the particular curriculum.

3. If enough SCCs are available to choose from, a student can spend a year in law, a year in culinary arts and hospitality, and a year in medical, and not choose any of these as a career. But he or she might still find these experiences provocative and life changing.

When course designers create a story, they must determine a set of tasks to be accomplished and decide how students will approach these assigned tasks. This is where the traditional notions of teaching must change.

When books were placed in classrooms, they were not simply read aloud to the assembled students. (Actually, they were at the beginning, hence the word *lecture*, which is Latin for *to read*.) New teaching methodologies evolved that were more appropriate to classrooms, and books became supplemental materials for teachers. Different media require different methods.

A great deal of work is required to build a realistic environment that enables practice and failure. A computer is not required to do this, but it makes life easier. If you want to build an airplane and make it fly, you could do so in your backyard. However, doing it on a computer allows you to build a much more powerful airplane.

Teamwork and mentoring are essential in an SCC. Working alone is not as fun. Conversations amongst students working on the same problem facilitate thinking. Conversations with a mentor help when students are stuck. Teamwork promotes critical thinking and collaboration skills. The *sine qua non* of the SCC is the continued improvement of a work product. Teachers evaluate the work, but their intent is to make students try again and do it better. Teachers don't just stand up and talk. Instead, they provide guidance and point students toward the help they need.

Issues arise in the daily lives of every adult that simply aren't taught in school, but these issues would naturally be part of any reasonable curriculum. For example, working with Columbia University, Socratic Arts built an SCC for running a day-care center so students could learn something about raising children instead of listening to lectures on developmental psychology. The Institute for the Learning Sciences built a high school-level SCC about working in a medical clinic so students could observe real-life injuries and illnesses and determine how to address them. This was part of a full-year course that immersed students in the world of medicine and health.

How SCCs Motivate

Motivation is an integral part of memory. It's difficult to learn what you know you will never use. You can memorize facts, but knowledge only is retained through practice. A doctor dealing with a troubling case tries to recall similar cases and asks other doctors about similar cases. The doctor tries to learn from his or her own experience or from the experience of others. Therefore, memory drives all knowledge.

The desire of any teacher is to have students come away from their class with new information and knowledge stored in their memories. Teachers may not look at it this way, but they are hoping that students remember what they teach. Most courses fail to change memory in any significant way. I can recall the words *entente cordiale* from my high school history course. I had an idea of what it meant, but in a deep sense, it meant nothing to me. I remember the words, although I was not really concerned with the causes of World War I then or now. But I recall getting a score of ninety on the test. (This had never happened to me before in a history course, which is why I remember it. My memory was altered by the surprise of getting a good grade in history, not by anything about history.) The material we memorize for tests usually doesn't stay in our memories for long.

Now, compare this with exams that assess whether someone can do a job that they already do. If that test is a good test, no studying should be required. We needn't study for the driving part of the driver's test when we apply for a new license. However, we might have to study for the written part because the knowledge being tested isn't information we use every day. All employees who do their job well should know most of the answers to any reasonable question about their job. If not, then the test is bad. The reason for this is easy enough—practice makes perfect. We don't forget experiences, but we do forget facts we don't use. "You will need it later" is not a motivating explanation.

An effective SCC motivates or builds on motivation that is inherently there in the first place. The job of a course designer is to create that motivation. For example, at Northwestern, we developed an art history course to prove this point. Students played the role of detectives trying to discover if a Rembrandt was actually a forgery. The students had fun and learned about art history. Did it matter? I am not sure that it did. It was entertaining, though. We also created a number of SCCs in history just to prove that students can be excited to learn, because the decisions they must make are interesting as well as the roles they play. We asked students to produce a television news show about events that took place twenty years earlier. If you teach history that way within an SCC, it is fun and students are motivated to learn.

How SCCs Encourage Learning by Doing

How much of what adults learn in school can they apply to their daily lives? I raised children, developed theories of how computers and people learn, negotiated various business deals, ran companies, negotiated personal relationships, and so on. Which of these skills did I learn in school? None.

Formal education is rarely about doing, especially the doing you actually engage in as an adult. Formal education is about knowing, not doing. Doing requires constant practice, and I do not mean practicing for a multiple-choice test.

Most courses are preparation for doing that never takes place. When you learn to balance a chemical equation, you are practicing a skill you might need someday. But what percentage of the adult population actually ever balances a chemical equation? The number is absurdly small. Why do we learn to do it then? Charles Eliot said so. Sometimes, debating ideas—a kind of doing—does occur in a course. In most courses, however, there is usually no doing at all.

Zookeeper SCC

A good example of doing can take place in a zookeeper SCC. Students would learn about biology, medicine, health, social problems, economics, management, and law. Students also would learn to work in and eventually run their own simulated zoo. In this SCC, they would attempt the following tasks.

- Learn to help out in a real zoo, meeting real people and performing menial tasks

- Learn the basics of working in administration, working with the public, and to a minimal extent, working with the animals

- Create and run a simulated zoo, involving issues of management, economics, and life-and-death situations, both physical and ethical

- Understand and be able to explain issues regarding the health and care of the animals and their natural environments

- Learn about government regulations and how to attend to zoo visitors

The idea is to marry practice and science. Students would learn these skills in context. They would need sufficient mathematics to help make financial and scientific decisions, and they would confront social issues while working with the public.

Other Example SCCs

One can create SCCs easily enough. Children like television. Allow them to create and produce a television program. Children like vehicles. Have them help repair cars, or better yet, design them. Children like talking about their world. Invite them to run a magazine that writes about issues they care about. Any or all of these contexts can be used to teach the traditional subjects, but we actually needn't teach the traditional subjects at all. The science they learn in these kinds of SCCs is more important than memorizing a physics formula. In SCCs, students who have given up on school find themselves interested once again when the subject matter looks real and the activities are meaningful.

School can be fun if we make it fun. Motivation is easy in a video game. Should school be more like a video game? Yes and no. An SCC is not a game. It is a serious exercise meant to be a memorable experience that involves hard work. When we work at something meaningful for a long time, we remember it.

Chapter 5

The Virtual Experiential High School

Education is an admirable thing, but it is well to remember from time to time that nothing that is worth learning can be taught.

—Oscar Wilde

What if students could do whatever they wanted in high school? It is easy to dismiss this idea out of hand because it seems so ridiculous. How would that work? How would students learn the right content? How can students know what they should be learning? I know the objections. Now, let's take the idea seriously anyway.

Let's imagine the virtual experiential high school (VEHS). This school would offer a new kind of curriculum designed to prepare students for the world of work as well as the possibility of college entry. Its primary focus would be offering new kinds of curricula that teach immediately useful, employable skills to successful graduates. These new curricula would be offered online, allowing students to work from home, the library, or dedicated school sites away from the distractions and difficulties of the typical classroom. Or, students could go to a school where they could have this kind of experience.

John Adams once said, "There are two types of education . . . One should teach us how to make a living, and the other how to live" (John Adams Historical Society, n.d.). The VEHS would do both. It would use a curriculum meant to simulate experiences in the real world. In this curriculum, experiences are the medium of instruction within a story in which students play roles in the real world. Assignments are clear and precise, with required deliverables at every step.

For example, in an entrepreneurship curriculum, students might be asked to write a business plan for their fictional company within a two-week timeframe. On the web, students would find a detailed description of the company they are supposed to create. Mentors would guide students toward ways to discover information about the market they are entering, the competition, and capital requirements. They would read books or hear stories from experts about writing a business plan. They would turn in a simple proposal in the first days and receive immediate feedback. Mentors would help students every step of the way. Using social media tools, students would work in teams to delegate the work and then meet to hash out the issues. Finally, students would create and submit a preliminary plan, and mentors would give feedback and advice for improving that plan. Students would then submit the plan to an expert. After this step, students would move on to the next project, building on what they just learned, for example, developing a website for their new company.

The VEHS would offer more than one hundred full-year curricula. These employment-oriented curricula would include courses such as medical technology, music technology, filmmaking, criminal investigation, graphic arts, computer programming, clothing design, television production, culinary arts and hospitality, and law. Experts would be enlisted to help create stories, establish the tasks for students to complete, and support students when they need help.

Students would have virtual experiences in their field of choice, spending a year working within a fictional story that has been created for them in a field that interests them. These experiences would be structured so that those who chose to pursue specific employable skills (such as training to be a paralegal, computer animation artist, or sound technician) would be employable immediately after graduation. In addition, the curricula would be structured so that the basics—such as communication (written and oral); reasoning; human relations; time management; deadlines; procedures; and relevant mathematics, science, and technology—are taught in context at every step of each curriculum. After completing a year's work, students would be ready to learn more, perhaps to apprentice during the summer using what they learned. Or, they might decide that the experience was not for them, and they should try something else.

Graduation from the VEHS would occur when the student completed four full-year curricula chosen from one hundred possibilities and taken in any order. Students could choose any curricula that interest them. Employers would sign up and agree to take students who have done well in the job-oriented curricula. Colleges would learn to deal with it. They might resist it at first, but they don't easily turn down bright, motivated students who have a good sense of what they want to learn.

Proposed Curricula for the VEHS

Following are thirty proposed curricula for the VEHS. It is easy enough to imagine more.

1. Law
2. Fashion
3. Civil engineering
4. Robotics
5. Computer programming
6. Medicine / health care
7. Nursing
8. Construction
9. Television production
10. Veterinary medicine
11. Investment banking

12. Aircraft design

13. Architecture

14. Biotechnology lab

15. Filmmaking

16. Entrepreneurship

17. Parenting and child care

18. Hotel management

19. Culinary arts and hospitality

20. Graphic arts

21. Real estate

22. Criminal justice

23. Music technology

24. Sports management

25. Landscape architecture

26. Financial planning

27. Urban transit

28. Engineering

29. Automobile design

30. Social work

All of these curricula would be delivered primarily online; however, when real-world experience is needed, teaching could move to an appropriate venue. Each curriculum would start with a story such as the following.

> You have been asked to help as an assistant in the next television production, criminal investigation, computer graphics art fair, and so on. Here is a task you can do in one week if you learn some of the basics. Here is where to start. You have been given some books and articles to read and some very simple assignments to complete. A mentor is available to help you. When you have completed the first simple tasks, you will be ready to join your team to deliver your work. You have ten days. Ask for help whenever you need it.

In such a project-oriented environment, students work with each other and with mentors to attempt tasks in a given field. Gradually, the assignments get more complex. As the complexity increases, students may have to learn a range of skills outside of their field. For example, they may be asked to prepare a budget for a project, perform a cost–benefit analysis, give a presentation, or write a proposal. Mentors would offer help with writing, reasoning, mathematics, and so on, in addition to giving specific advice about work in their field or industry.

The online experience allows for many mentors to give advice and for like-minded students who may not be physically present to work in teams. At the end of one year, graduates from a given curriculum will have a year's worth of experience in a given field. Because these experiences are designed with potential employers as part of the design team, the result should be immediate employment for those who seek it and curiosity about the next challenge for those who choose to enter a given field. In other words, students start at the beginning and can choose to go as far as their interests and abilities take them. If they want to continue doing what they have been doing, they would be free to do that.

For students interested in working in the fashion industry, for example, course designers would create a story involving fashion-related elements such as design, delivery, marketing, and business management as well as the use of materials and design tools.

The same elements would apply in the film industry. But here, the team approach becomes more significant. While students might aspire to become filmmakers, others might be interested in jobs such as lighting or sound engineering. A team would be comprised of students with each of these interests, but they would play many roles in order to learn about each job in the course of the year. At the end, some students might choose to go to work immediately, while others might to choose to study filmmaking in college.

Notice that very few of the proposed curricula are subjects studied in college, much less in high school. The idea here is to abandon the 1892 curriculum entirely and replace it with experiences that might result in employment or in students deciding to attend college. Either way, students would be having fun and working hard, learning skills that actually matter in the real world.

Goals of the Curricula

The goal of each curriculum, in addition to the more obvious stated goals, is to teach the following.

- Reasoning
- Human relations
- Communication
- Specific job skills
- Organization
- Meeting deadlines
- Time management
- Following procedures
- Creativity

- Taking initiative
- Decision making
- Value judgments
- Ethics
- Prioritizing
- Scientific principles
- Economic principles
- Basic mathematics

None of these skills are taught directly. Not every student needs the same training or the same information. Some students easily take initiative. Others have no trouble with deadlines. Some people need public speaking skills, and others do not. A proper education experience is individually tailored.

The only reason for not reframing education in this way is money; but in an online world, that reason becomes much less significant. A country that can devote $5 billion to fighting Ebola can devote a much smaller amount of money to changing education to offer a more relevant student experience (The Advisory Board Company, 2014).

There is really no excuse for our inability to offer choices. We just need to ask students what they would like to learn and ask employers what skills they want new hires to possess. The question is not what academic subjects university professors want students to learn. Today, college is seen as a necessity because high school has become so useless. But college has become useless too.

The basics—that stuff everyone must know before they go to college or after they graduate college—don't really exist. Students do not need to know anything in particular before going to college, except for reading, writing, and reasoning their way through an argument or issue. And after college, they know whatever they happen to pay attention to and remember.

However, students do need to know how to work, deliver what is expected of them, interact and collaborate with peers, and analyze issues that they have determined are important. If a student is interested in business, let him or her participate in business with our guidance and help. Bill Gates doesn't have a business degree. In fact, he doesn't even have a college degree. Success in life is dependent on abilities and passion, not degrees.

The Future

The days are gone when faculty just teach what they have always taught and get away with it. High schools and colleges will begin to design courses (or better yet, recreate experiences) focused on student needs and interests, and that eventually, lead to employment. There is no need for thousands of colleges and who knows how many high schools anymore. Once we do it right, and students have the choice to enroll anywhere they want because location no longer matters, schools that refuse to change will cease to exist.

The critical next steps for changing education and taking it to the next level are two-fold: (1) design curricula well, and (2) convince those in charge to stop preventing change. Students do not have to be convinced about change. Students will probably have to work harder than ever before because teachers will expect them to submit actual deliverables. They won't be able to just get by with cramming the night before the test. They can stop thinking about grades, listening to lectures, and showing up for class at 8:00 a.m. Students will realize that learning can be, as it usually is in real life, relevant and fun.

I conclude with a quote by Max Sonderby. Max was a teacher's assistant in the first SCC-based master's degree program designed by my team at Carnegie Mellon and Socratic Arts. It was offered at Carnegie Mellon's Silicon Valley Campus in 2002. The year before, he had finished a master's degree at Carnegie Mellon using the typical classroom-based approach to education.

> I am almost jealous, in a way. I see that [students] are gaining skills more readily than I gained them in the program, which I attended in Pittsburgh on Carnegie Mellon's campus. So . . . they get exposure to things that we just talked about in a lecture hall . . . They are actually doing it, implementing, building software, putting designs into practice, whereas we mostly just did homework and talked about it in a lecture hall . . . So, I am jealous in that respect, but it's also a lot more work, but that work definitely pays off for the students. (as cited in Schank, 2015)

References and Resources

The Advisory Board Company. (2014, December 15). *The daily briefing: Senate passes budget deal with funding for Ebola fight.* Accessed at www.advisory.com/daily-briefing/2014/12/15 /senate-passes-cromnibus on March 15, 2014.

Burian, P. (2012, June 25). Defending the humanities. *Inside Higher Ed.* Accessed at www.insidehighered.com/views/2012 /06/25/essay-how-defend-humanities on March 15, 2014.

CBS News. (2014, September 16). *Rewriting history? Texas tackles textbook debate.* Accessed at www.cbsnews.com/news/rewriting -history-texas-tackles-textbook-debate on April 2, 2015.

Cho, A. (2014, October 2). Bill Gates addresses issues in higher education. *Cornell Daily Sun.* Accessed at http://cornellsun.com /blog/2014/10/02/gates-addresses-cornellians-in-bailey on April 2, 2015.

The College Board. (2015a). *Full SAT practice test.* Accessed at https:// sat.collegeboard.org/practice/sat-practice-test on March 15, 2014.

The College Board. (2015b). *SAT subject test practice: U.S. history.* Accessed at https://sat.collegeboard.org/practice/sat-subject-test -preparation/us-history on July 17, 2014.

The College Board. (2015c). *SAT subject test practice: Biology E/M.* Accessed at https://sat.collegeboard.org/practice/sat-subject-test -preparation/biology-em on June 5, 2014.

The College Board. (2015d). *SAT subject test practice: Physics.* Accessed at https://sat.collegeboard.org/practice/sat-subject-test -preparation/physics on June 5, 2014.

Committee of Ten. (1892). Report of the Committee of Ten. In House of Representatives, *Report of the secretary of the interior; being part of the message and documents communicated to the two houses of Congress at the beginning of the second session of the Fifty-Third Congress* (Vol. 5, part 2, pp. 1415–1447). Washington, DC: U.S. Government Printing Office.

Dewey, J. (1910). *How we think.* Chicago: D. C. Heath and Company.

Dewey, J. (1916). *Democracy and education: An introduction to the philosophy of education.* New York: Macmillan.

Dewey, J. (1938). *Experience and education* (60th anniversary ed.). Indianapolis, IN: Kappa Delta Pi.

Dexter, E. G. (1906). Ten years' influence of the report of the Committee of Ten. *The School Review, 14*(4), 254–269.

Doyle, A. (n.d.). *Top 15 kids' dream jobs.* Accessed at http://jobsearch .about.com/od/kids/ss/top-15-kids-dream-jobs.htm#step-heading on February 15, 2015.

Einstein, A. (1956). *Out of my later years.* New York: Citadel Press.

Fly Away Simulation. (2010, July 12). *Flight simulator technology through the years.* Accessed at https://web.archive.org/web /20111012134549/http://flyawaysimulation.com/news/4045 /flight-simulator-technology-through-years/ on January 20, 2015.

Gatto, J. T. (2009). *Weapons of mass instruction: A schoolteacher's journey through the dark world of compulsory schooling.* Gabriola Island, British Columbia, Canada: New Society.

Goodman, P. (1964). *Compulsory mis-education and the community of scholars.* New York: Horizon Press.

Harvard University. (n.d.). *Choosing courses.* Accessed at https:// college.harvard.edu/admissions/preparing-college/choosing -courses on April 2, 2015.

Hertzberg, H. W. (1988, February). Foundations: The 1892 Committee of Ten. *Social Education, 52*(2), 144–145.

Holt, J. (1969). *The underachieving school.* New York: Pitman Publishing.

Illich, I. (1971). *Deschooling society*. London: Marion Boyars.

John Adams Historical Society. (n.d.). *John Adams quotes on education*. Accessed at www.john-adams-heritage.com /quotes/ on March 15, 2014.

Layton, L. (2014, March 14). Bill Gates calls on teachers to defend Common Core. *Washington Post*. Accessed at www .washingtonpost.com/local/education/bill-gates-calls-on-teachers -to-defend-common-core/2014/03/14/395b130a-aafa-11e3 -98f6-8e3c562f9996_story.html on March 17, 2015.

Leitch, A. (1978). *A Princeton companion*. Princeton, NJ: Princeton University Press.

Mencken, H. L. (1949). *A Mencken chrestomathy*. New York: Knopf.

National Education Association of the United States. (1894). *Report of the Committee of Ten on secondary school studies: With the reports of the conferences arranged by the committee*. Accessed at https:// books.google.com/books?id=PfcBAAAAYAAJ&pg=PA3&lpg =PA3&hl=en#v=onepage&q&f=false on November 3, 2012.

National STEM Centre. (2012, March). *Seven of the top 10 children's dream jobs are in STEM*. Accessed at www.nationalstemcentre .org.uk/news/seven-of-the-top-10-childrens-dream-jobs-are-in -stem on March 17, 2015.

Plato. (1892). Theaetetus. In *The dialogues of Plato* (B. Jowett, Trans.; 3rd ed., Vol. 4, pp. 107–280). New York: Oxford University Press.

Postman, N., & Weingartner, C. (1969). *Teaching as a subversive activity*. New York: Delacorte Press.

Reimer, E. W. (1971). *School is dead: An essay on alternatives in education*. London: Penguin.

Romano, L. (2014, September 30). Transcript: Bill Gates' lessons from leaders interview. *Politico*. Accessed at www.politico .com/story/2014/09/transcript-bill-gates-lessons-from-leaders -interview-111470_Page3.html on April 2, 2015.

Schank, R. (2015, January 24). Why do we give lectures? Why does anyone attend them? [Web log post]. Accessed at http:// educationoutrage.blogspot.com/2015/01/why-do-we-give -lectures-why-does-anyone.html on March 25, 2015.

Sears, J. B., & Henderson, A. (1957). *Cubberley of Stanford and his contribution to American education.* Stanford, CA: Stanford University Press.

Simon, S. (2014, September 29). Bill Gates plugs Common Core, Arne Duncan. *Politico.* Accessed at www.politico.com /story/2014/09/bill-gates-common-core-111426.html on March 17, 2015.

Sorkin, A. R. (2014, September 5). So Bill Gates has this idea for a history class . . . *New York Times Magazine.* Accessed at www .nytimes.com/2014/09/07/magazine/so-bill-gates-has-this-idea -for-a-history-class.html on March 17, 2015.

Stutz, T. (2014, September 16). Right, left blast new Texas textbooks. *Dallas Morning News.* Accessed at www.dallasnews.com/news /education/headlines/20140916-right-left-blast-new-texas -textbooks.ece on March 17, 2015.

Weiss, J. (2015, February 16). *Officially, Texas can't say the cost of standardized tests through the decades.* Accessed at http:// educationblog.dallasnews.com/2015/02/officially-texas-cant-say -the-cost-of-standardized-tests-through-the-decades.html/ on June 5, 2014.

Solutions for Modern Learning

Solutions Series: Solutions for Modern Learning engages K–12 educators in a powerful conversation about learning and schooling in the connected world. In a short, reader-friendly format, these books challenge traditional thinking about education and help to develop the modern contexts teachers and leaders need to effectively support digital learners.

Claim Your Domain—And Own Your Online Presence
by Audrey Watters
BKF687

The End of School as We Know It
by Bruce Dixon
BKF692

Freedom to Learn
by Will Richardson
BKF688

Gearing Up for Learning Beyond K–12
by Bryan Alexander
BKF693

Make School Meaningful—And Fun!
by Roger C. Schank
BKF686

The New Pillars of Modern Teaching
by Gayle Allen
BKF685

Wait! Your professional development journey doesn't have to end with the last pages of this book.

We realize improving student learning doesn't happen overnight. And your school or district shouldn't be left to puzzle out all the details of this process alone.

No matter where you are on the journey, we're committed to helping you get to the next stage.

Take advantage of everything from **custom workshops** to **keynote presentations** and **interactive web and video conferencing**. We can even help you develop an action plan tailored to fit your specific needs.

Let's get the conversation started.

Call 888.763.9045 today.

solution-tree.com